Backpacking
Tips

Trail-Tested Wisdom from FalconGuide Authors

Edited by Bill and Russ Schneider

FALCON®

Helena, Montana

©1998 Falcon® Publishing, Inc., Helena, Montana
Printed in Canada.

1 2 3 4 5 6 7 8 9 0 TP 03 02 01 00 99 98

Illustrations by Todd Telander

Cover Photo: Cliff Leight

Library of Congress Cataloging-in-Publication Data

Backpacking tips / edited by Bill and Russ Schneider.
    p.   cm.
    1. Backpacking. 2. Hiking. I. Schneider, Bill. II. Schneider, Russ.
GV199.6.B34 1998
796.51—dc21
                                          98-3329
                                            CIP

CAUTION:

Outdoor recreation can be dangerous, including hiking and backpacking. Everyone who goes into the wilderness or backcountry assumes some risk and responsibility for his or her own actions and safety.

The information contained in this book is a summary of both authors' personal experiences, research, review of existing literature on backpacking, guiding experience, and conversations with backpacking experts. However, neither this book (nor any other book) can assure your safety from the elements. Nor can this book (or any other book) replace sound judgment and good decision-making skills, which will greatly reduce the risks of going into the wilderness.

Learn as much as possible from this book and other sources of information, and prepare for the unexpected. Be cautious. The reward will be a safer and more enjoyable experience.

Contents

Thank you for supporting Falcon as we promote responsible outdoor recreation.

Acknowledgments

Special thanks to all of the FalconGuide authors for contributing tips to this project on short notice including: Ron Adkison, Donna Ikenberry, Polly Burke, Bill Cunningham, Bert Gildart, Jane Gildart, Bill Hunger, Bruce Grubbs, Rhonda Ostertag, George Ostertag, Will Harmon, Gilbert Preston, and Fred Barstad. Thanks to the following Glacier Wilderness Guides for helping with the review of this book, especially John Gray, Jan Metzmaker, Carolyn Beecher, and Denny Gignoux. In addition, thanks to Glacier Wilderness Guides for providing a knowledge-enhancing environment. Moreover, thanks to Erin Turner and Larissa Berry for producing this book on a rigorous schedule.

Introduction

Backpacking can be the best therapy for everyday ills of stress, overstimulation, and the fast pace of society. Backpacking can give you time to think, a feeling of self-reliance, a deeper understanding of nature, and bring you closer to your companions. Unfortunately, backpacking is not easy, especially the first time you venture out.

You can go into the backcountry in shorts and a T-shirt and with a little food and usually survive; but if it isn't warm and sunny every day, your trip will be miserable. You could also die. Exposure to the elements can lead to life-threatening situations—hypothermia, heat stroke, dehydration, shock, and even death. A safe trip is always a more enjoyable trip, even if it is not as memorable. Everyone who survived the *Titanic* disaster surely had a memorable trip, but they probably didn't enjoy it. Keeping everyone warm and comfortable might convince your companions to go backpacking with you again.

Backpacking is not about having the most expensive gear, hiking the most miles humanly possible, carrying the most weight, or never seeing another person along the trail; it is about enjoying nature, exploring with friends, and learning to appreciate the world in its natural state.

The tips contained in this book can help you avoid common mistakes and refine your existing knowledge of backpacking. The tips came primarily from FalconGuide authors. Tips without credit lines are from either Bill or Russ. These tips are for everybody, but not all of them will work for everybody every time; pick and choose the techniques and suggestions that work for you. Develop your own tips. One thing we discovered is that each FalconGuide author has his or her own way of doing things. You will develop your own style, too. These tips should help you do just that.

The Tips

The Boy Scouts of America have been guided for decades by what is perhaps the single best piece of safety advice—Be Prepared! For starters, this means carrying survival and first-aid materials, proper clothing, a compass, and a topographic map, and knowing how to use them.

❦

Tell somebody where you are going and when you plan to return. File your "flight plan," including alternatives to it and which car you are taking (with license plate number), with a friend or relative before taking off, and call him or her immediately upon your return.

❦

Before you head into the backcountry, highlight your route on a map and leave it with a friend or at a local ranger station.—Will Harmon, *Wild Country Companion*

PLANNING

Planning saves valuable time better spent hiking. Wildlife management, fires, high water, road construction, and other factors can change conditions unexpectedly in areas where you want to hike, so you want to plan an alternative route.

❧

Have several backup trips lined up within the region of your intended trek. This allows you to alter your hike based on weather, insect, and trail or road conditions. If you expect rain, take the hike up a forested valley; if mosquitoes are voracious, hike a dry peak.—Rhonda and George Ostertag, *Hiking New York*

❧

Pick a hike appropriate to your level of experience. Beginners should try a short overnighter before attempting an extended trip. Try to keep your first trip to about 5 miles or less one-way.

❧

Engage all participants in picking and planning a hike. For a happier group, each individual should be invited to provide input on length, terrain, and duration.—Polly Burke, *Hiking California's Desert Parks*

❦

For early spring trips, seek out trails at lower elevations on south-facing slopes. These areas shed their snow and dry out earlier than other areas.—Will Harmon, *Hiking Alberta*

❦

Check with the land-management agency to make sure your route follows maintained trails and, if so, find out when the trail was last cleared of downfall. Unmaintained trails with lots of downfall make travel much slower, more strenuous and sometimes dangerous. If you anticipate hiking off-trail or on a trail that has not been maintained for years, expect slow going and difficult route-finding.

❦

For several reasons, the prime season for hiking in most of North America is mid-July through September. Hungry mosquitoes and black flies await hikers in most areas in June and even into July. In addition, with the deep snowfall in the high country, you can't hike many high-altitude trails until mid-July; and in some low-altitude areas, trails remain wet and mushy, and high water makes fords dangerous until then. Southern states and desert areas offer great hiking in early spring and early fall, so if you are willing to travel, you can hike almost all year long.

CONDITIONING

Hiking and backpacking are by their very nature strenuous outdoor activities. Consult a physician before going on a backpacking trip.

❧

Try easy hikes with your pack fully loaded to get in shape before you try extended treks.

❧

A combination of weight training, exercise machines, and running or cross-country skiing during the winter months can help you get in shape for hiking season.

GUIDEBOOKS AND MAPS

Guidebooks can help you locate an area you want

to visit and provide detailed trip planning and trail descriptions, but a guidebook doesn't take the place of a good topographic map.

❧

A GOOD GUIDEBOOK SHOULD INCLUDE:
Current information, i.e., check the copyright date.
Clear instructions on how to get to the trailhead, including road conditions.
Recommendations of which maps to purchase or copy.
Information on special regulations or permits required for the area.
A rating system for the difficulty of a trail including information or charts on large elevation changes or potential hazards such as river fords.

❧

Buy a guidebook on the area you plan to visit early in the planning stages of your trip. It may help you decide which hike you want to take, not just what the trail will be like when you get there.

❧

Half the fun of planning a backpacking trip is poring over maps, finding the most remote places, and dreaming about visiting them.

❧

United States Geological Survey (USGS) 7.5-minute topographic, Trails Illustrated, Green Trails, and Earthwalk Press are the best general maps to carry. The USDA Forest Service (USDAFS) or Bureau of Land Management (BLM) recreation maps may be the only maps with road numbers and exact trailhead locations for a particular area.

❧

Many topographic maps are outdated; while still accurate in topography, years of logging and other development can change the surface of the land. Updated guidebooks and information from local management agencies offer the most accurate guidelines.—Bill Hunger, *Hiking Wyoming*

❧

You can find USGS, USDAFS, BLM, and Canadian topographic maps at many sporting goods stores or at visitor centers in the area you visit. Inquire with local management agencies about other available maps, but you should always have some type of topographic map.

❦

You can order topographic maps directly from the USGS and Canada Map Office at the following addresses:

USGS Information Services	Canada Map Office
P.O. Box 25286	130 Bentley Road
Federal Center	Ottawa, Ontario
Denver, CO 80225	Canada
1-800-USA-MAPS	K1A 0E9
http://mapping.usgs.gov	1-800-465-6277

❦

To save money, if your local library has a complete file of local topographic maps, photocopy the relevant topographic map(s) or map sections covering your route. Use a dark setting on the copier, tape sections together, and store in a zip-locked bag for ready reference.—Bill Cunningham, *Wild Utah*

❦

Be realistic about estimating mileage on a map. Trails are never straight, even if they appear so on a map.

TYPES OF TRIPS

Loop trips start and finish at the same trailhead, with no (or very little) retracing of your steps.

❦

Out-and-back trips take you to a destination, then back to the trailhead. They are logistically simple, but limit the amount of scenery.

❦

Base camp trips involve hiking into an area, setting up camp in the same place for several days, and taking shorter day trips from camp, which allow for enjoyable fishing, climbing, and day hiking in remote areas. Plan a long first day of hiking to a location that offers a variety of intriguing day trips.

❦

Shuttle trips are point-to-point hikes that require two vehicles (one left at both ends of the trail) or a prearranged pickup at a designated time and place.

❦

When avoiding a car shuttle by doing a one-way hike in two groups, each party should carry keys to both cars. Bad weather or unforeseen problems may prevent a mid-trip key swap. Agree on a post-trip meeting point ahead of time.—Bruce Grubbs, *Hiking Great Basin National Park*

PERMITS

Backcountry use regulations help preserve the natural landscape and protect visitors. Many national parks, state parks, and, increasingly, national forests require that you obtain a permit before camping in popular areas.

❦

Take advantage of advance reservation systems to get the best sites, but expect to pay a small fee for that permit. If you cannot get one in advance, you can usually get one at a visitor center in the area you are visiting, but it might not be for your most preferred campsite.

❦

Use the Internet to search for information on your

destination, especially regarding fees, permits, and special regulations, which often change yearly.

✦

In addition to backcountry campsite permits, many areas now charge fees for parking at popular trailheads.

EQUIPMENT

Don't get too caught up in the gear. Too much expensive gear can break your checkbook and heavy high-tech gadgets can break your back. Spend money on rain gear (7–9% of your gear weight), a good tent (10–14% of your gear weight), backpack (10–15% of your gear weight), and a warm sleeping bag (9–11% of your gear weight). Otherwise, moderately priced items will suffice.

✦

Test gear before buying it. Many outdoor-equipment stores offer rental programs so you can do this.

✦

Buy backpacks and boots from a shop that can fit you properly.

❦

Search the Internet for online product reviews of gear you want to purchase before spending the money.

❦

It is not really that special, but one piece of equipment you definitely need is a good supply of zip-locked bags. This handy invention is perfect for keeping food smell to a minimum and helps keep food from spilling on your pack, clothing, or other gear.

FOOD

You can make your trip much less enjoyable by fretting too much over food. Perhaps the most common option is freeze-dried food. It carries little smell, and it comes in convenient envelopes that allow you to cook it by merely adding boiling water. This means you don't have cooking pans to wash or store.

❦

Dry pre-packed meals (often pasta- or rice-based) offer an affordable alternative to freeze-dried foods.

You can supplement these meals by bringing pita bread, bagels, tortillas, and dehydrated salsa. Do not bring salt; most backpacking food already has plenty of salt.

✦

Take plenty of snacks. In case you don't bring enough other food, you'll have something to keep you going.

✦

Avoid fresh fruit (because it's heavy), and canned meats and fish when camping in bear country.

✦

Get calories from the following sources: 40% from carbohydrates, 30% from protein, and 30% from fat. On trips above 10,000 feet, you should increase your carbohydrate intake to 70% of your calories.—Gilbert Preston, M.D., *Wilderness First Aid*

✦

Make a tasty backpacking dinner by filling burrito shells with couscous or tabouli. Add some fresh vegetables on the first and second nights, and eat like a queen.—Donna Ikenberry, *Hiking Oregon*

❧

If you are heavily into extended backpacking trips, consider purchasing a food dehydrator to make your own food. You should be able to recoup the cost by not having to purchase expensive, commercially available dehydrated foods.—Jane and Bert Gildart, *Hiking South Dakota's Black Hills Country*

❧

On extended trips, purposely pack one meal that is larger than needed (i.e., twice what you expect to eat in an average meal) and save it for later in the trip, when you are sure to eat it all.

STOVES

If you generally camp in mild climates, consider using butane canister stoves. They light easily, burn hot, and are lightweight.

❧

If you plan to hike and camp in areas with colder temperatures with the possibility of summer snow, it is probably better to use a white-gas stove. Technology may make butane stoves more usable at colder temperatures, and it may be possible in the future to forgo white-gas-burning stoves. However, using white gas arguably produces less wasted metal canisters than butane.

Regardless of what stove you purchase the most important thing you need to know is how to use it. After you purchase a stove, take it apart, put it back together, and see if you can purchase replacement parts. Start it, clean it, repair it, and light it prior to leaving home. You can make most stoves work if you keep them clean, maintained, and know how to fix them. You may have to rebuild all or part of a stove after a while. This is especially true of shaker jet models.

Follow starting directions exactly. If it says pump 25 times, pump 25 times.

COOK KITS

Pack cooking utensils, scrubby, soap, matches with strike strip and food screen in the cook kit, so you always have them handy.

❦

If you plan to cook pancakes, do not use the lid of your aluminum cook kit; carry a lightweight non-stick pan or consider a different breakfast.

❦

Bring a screen to filter food chunks out of dishwater before broadcasting it at least 100 feet away from water. Put the food scraps in the garbage and pack it out.

CLOTHING

Do not leave home without essential clothing for cold weather, even if the forecast looks good. The two most essential items are a rain suit and extra wool sweater or fleece jacket. Other items are a little less important depending upon the climate, the length of your stay, the season, and the distance back to your vehicle. It is easy to carry too much, but it can be deadly to carry too little.

❧

Once you reach the top of a climb, take off the wet layer of clothing directly next to your skin and replace it with a dry layer.

❧

You might think that polarfleece is lighter than wool. This is not always true. When I weighed a wool sweater and a fleece jacket of the same size and thickness, there was less than an ounce difference. However, if both get wet, the fleece will be lighter and will dry faster.

❧

When packing your clothes, remember to place your varied layers where you can get them easily. The polarfleece doesn't do you any good if it is at the bottom of your pack and is too much trouble to get to.—Polly Burke, *Hiking California's Desert Parks*

❧

For desert hiking areas, strive for light, white-cotton shirts, pants, and hats, but remember to bring warm clothing for the nighttime. Clear desert skies do not hold the daytime warmth.

SHOES AND BOOTS

Trail-running or trail-hiking shoes are low-impact, light on your feet, and cheaper to replace than full leather boots. However, weak, injury-prone ankles may fare better with the stability of a full leather boot.

❦

Hike your shoes dry to prevent them from shrinking.

❦

If your boots start to leak in bad weather, or you are using lightweight boots or running shoes that are not waterproof, use a couple of plastic bags as outer socks, and put your shoes on over them to help keep your feet dry. Leave the bags loose over your toes so you will not punch holes in them. Gallon-sized zip-locked bags work well.—Bruce Grubbs, *Hiking Oregon's Three Sisters Wilderness*

❦

Consider wearing waterproof breathable socks and running shoes for wet hiking. Any boot, no matter how expensive, will not protect your feet from wetness in a heavy rain.

❧

Always bring extra socks.

TENTS

Practice setting up your tent in the back yard or your living room before you go backpacking, so you will not have to struggle with unfamiliar seams, poles, and stakes in pouring rain.

❧

Tents are a big portion of both the weight and expense of backpacking. Cheap tents can make for a miserable and dangerous experience, while expensive tents usually are not worth the price. We do not recommend single-wall tents. You are better off sleeping under a well-strung tarp.

❧

A lightweight nylon tarp can also be a survival item. It can be quickly erected to protect from rain, hail, sleet, and snow.—Jane and Bert Gildart, *Hiking South Dakota's Black Hills Country*

❧

Remember that four-season tents are often four pounds heavier than suitable three-season tents.

Even if you think that you might use your tent all four seasons, you might want an additional, lighter tent for summer use.

❦

Get a freestanding tent or dome tent that requires few tent stakes. Tent stakes have a tendency to disappear and you should be able to set up a tent without them.

❦

Get a tent with a fly that completely protects all entrances and windows, and preferably with a good vestibule or awning for dry storage outside the tent.

❦

Get a stuff sack that is much larger than the size of the rolled-up tent. This speeds packing time and prevents wear and tear from shoving a too-large rolled up tent into a too-small stuff sack.

SLEEPING BAGS AND PADS

A sleeping bag is a good place to lay down some extra dollars. It could save your life. Synthetic sleeping bags tend to be a little heavier than down-filled bags. Synthetic bags, will, however, retain insulating value when wet, while down-filled bags become useless. We recommend a 20-degree F bag or warmer. You can always cool off by unzipping it or sleeping on top.

❧

To assure that your sleeping bag stays dry in any weather, heavy-duty garbage bags make excellent liners for sleeping bag stuff sacks. Place the plastic bag inside your stuff sack, then stuff the sleeping bag inside and place a twist tie on after fully compressing the bag.—Fred Barstad, *Hiking Oregon's Eagle Cap Wilderness*

❧

For a pillow, stuff some clothes into your sleeping bag stuff sack, then zip your fleece vest or jacket around the outside of your makeshift pillow. This gives you a comfy pillow that is fluffy and soft on your face.

❧

When luxury camping, it may be worth it to carry an inflatable mattress with a chair cover. Foam pads are best for reducing weight, but they do not keep you as warm as air mattresses that hold a warm layer of air under you. If you plan to use only a thin foam pad, bring a slightly warmer sleeping bag.

BACKPACKS

Size matters. Do not buy a too-big pack; it will just induce you to carry more than you need.

❦

We recommend internal frame packs. External frame packs are suited to big-shouldered people; internal frame packs put the weight on your hips, where most of us have the big muscles.

❦

Internal Frame Packs vs. External Frame Packs	
More Padding	More Ventilation
More Capacity	Easier Access
More Expensive	More Durable
More Weight on Hips	More Weight on Shoulders

❦

Buy from a dealer who will honor your warranty for life. A pack should last you twenty years, even when heavily used.

❈

Make sure you fit the pack loaded with 50 pounds or so to get a realistic feel for how comfortable it will be on the trail. You should also make sure that your chest and belt straps are comfortable and allow sufficient tightening to distribute the load.

❈

The weight of your backpack, surprisingly, can be a good portion of your gear weight, 10–15%. Extended trip backpacks vary in weight from 4 to 8 pounds.

❈

Get a pack with some outside pockets for storing day-use items.

❈

Avoid built-in water bags. They are often difficult to fill with water or filter into. A good water bottle does not need fixing, is inexpensive to purchase or replace, and is easy to clean. Spend the money you could spend on an expensive hydration system on a better tent or sleeping bag.

The best way to adjust your pack is to have it fitted properly when you buy it. Pick a dealer who will measure your torso length and correctly adjust a fully loaded pack in the store. The diagram below includes tips for a properly fitted pack.

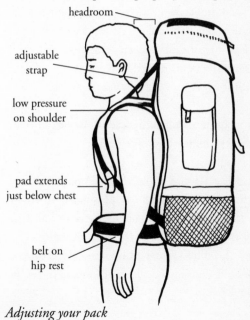

headroom

adjustable strap

low pressure on shoulder

pad extends just below chest

belt on hip rest

Adjusting your pack

PACKING YOUR PACK

Ideally you should carry no more than one-third of your body weight. Carrying too much can cause permanent damage to your body. If you are hiking with a group, you should be able to distribute community items. If you are responsible for a group, you may end up with more weight, but if you are frugal, you may be able to get your pack down to around 30 pounds. You can always reduce weight by omitting items related to comfort. Do not cut weight by leaving your rain gear at home.

❦

Use a cheap foam pad instead of heavier air mattresses (savings—10 ounces).

❦

Avoid heavy utility tools: a Swiss Army knife may be just as useful and lighter, -plus you never know when you might have to open a bottle of fine wine (utility tool—6 ounces, Swiss Army knife—3.5 ounces). Note: Lighter utility tools do exist, but they often don't include useful features of their full-size relatives.

❦

Pay close attention to the weight of items that make up a large percentage of the total, like your tent (10–14% of gear weight), sleeping bag (9–11% of gear weight), backpack (12% of gear weight), and food (13–14% of gear weight).

❦

Use iodine tablets instead of a water filter to treat water and carry some flavored drink mix to mask the taste (savings— 17.5 ounces).

❦

Save space and weight by eating out of your cup and bringing only one pan (savings—44 ounces).

❦

On short trips in mild climates, carry food that does not need to be cooked, such as fruit, nuts, cheese, tortillas, granola, and crackers. Save weight and chores by leaving the stove and gas at home (savings—63-plus ounces).—Will Harmon, *Wild Country Companion*

❦

Repackage food in plastic freezer or zip-locked bags and reduce the amount of garbage, cardboard, and packaging you carry into the backcountry (savings—10-plus ounces).—Will Harmon *Hiking Alberta*

❦

Packing your backpack is often frustrating and time-consuming, but it is always important. Strive to balance the weight of your pack from side to side and avoid sticking heavy objects, like your tent, on top or far away from your center of gravity. Pack items you might need during the day in an outside pocket or in the top of your pack.

❦

Think of the order of your chores once you reach camp and what things you will actually use on the trail. At camp, chores may occur in the following order: set up tent; throw in sleeping bag, pad, and clothes; then at the food prep area, begin cooking dinner after gathering all food bags from group members. To make this process efficient, strap the tent and pad on the outside of your pack and pack sleeping bag and clothes above cooking items. Items needed on the trail—such as rain gear, hat, gloves, fleece vest, snacks, sunglasses, sunscreen, bug dope, and first-aid kit—should either be in the top zippered portion of the pack, close to the top, or in an outside pocket.

Use mesh or nylon "ditty bags" to organize all small items into logical groups like personal kit and survival kit, and use them to split food into snacks, drinks, breakfast foods, and evening foods.

Several carabiners clipped to loops on the outside of your pack can be very handy for clipping your boots on for a stream crossing and tying down exterior items.—Fred Barstad, *Hiking Oregon's Mount Hood and Badger Creek Wilderness*

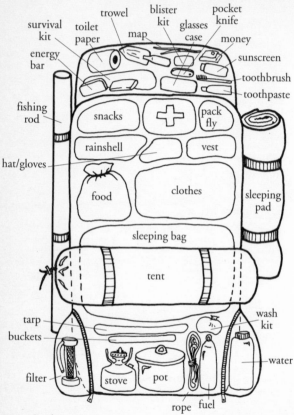

Packing your pack

❦

If you do not fill up your internal frame pack, stuff the top portion of the pack into the main portion. This makes your pack smaller and distributes weight more evenly.

TRAILHEADS

Make sure you have good directions to the trailhead before leaving for your hike.

❦

Check road conditions before leaving, and always inquire locally for current road conditions leading to the trailhead. Roads to backcountry trailheads are sometimes poorly maintained and are often winding dirt roads. Many trails start right from paved roads, especially in national parks, but others start from unpaved spur roads. Depending upon road conditions and the remoteness of the trailhead, you may or may not need a high-clearance vehicle or four-wheel-drive capacity.

❦

Save time by getting up early and driving to the trailhead before most tourists leave camp and clog the roads.

❦

Roadside assistance service provided by insurance companies often ends when the pavement ends, giving new meaning to "off-road." Get a clear description of your coverage from your insurance company.

❦

Do not expect the trailhead to be marked; quite often trailhead signs are victims of backcountry vandalism.

FOREIGN TRAILHEADS

Backpacking abroad requires extensive research and preparation beyond any guidebook.

❦

Be sure to start your passport and visa process at least six months in advance and find out as much as you can from books, government resources, the Internet, and embassies before going abroad.

❦

Avoid countries in the midst of political turmoil or war, and contact embassy officials in the country you intend to visit to inquire about any travel restrictions or warnings for potential visitors.

❦

If you are planning to enter exotic rain forests or deserts, learn about dangerous plants and animals common to those areas.

❦

For more information on obtaining a visa, contact

Office of Visa Services
Bureau of Consular Affairs
U.S. Department of State
2201 C Street N. W.
Washington, D.C. 20520

❦

If you are planning a trip out of North America, call the Center for Disease Control (CDC) in Atlanta (404-332-4559) for up-to-date recommendations on vaccinations.—Gilbert Preston M.D., *Wilderness First Aid*

VEHICLES AND KEYS

Place a hide-a-key somewhere on your vehicle in case you lose your keys and make sure all members of the group know where it is.

❧

Fasten your keys securely inside your pack.

❧

Instead of exchanging keys mid-trip, you can also just carry two sets of keys—one set for each group—and if no exchange is made, you can start either car.

❧

Unfortunately, trailhead crime is a concern, especially near urban areas. Lock your vehicle and try not to leave anything valuable inside.

❧

Deter trailhead theft by driving an old, beat-up car.

❧

Arrange to be picked up so you don't have to leave your vehicle at the trailhead.

❧

Empty most of the contents of your wallet or purse before leaving home. Take only essentials: an all-purpose credit card, driver's license, fishing license, and emergency cash. This reduces the headache of replacement should the wallet become lost or soaked in a river. The same frugal policy goes for

keys: car and house keys should do the ticket.—
Rhonda and George Ostertag, *Hiking Pennsylvania*

WEATHER

Probably the best way to predict the weather is to
listen to the forecast carefully and watch the general trend of weather. Your best source of weather
forecasts is The Weather Channel, and you can get
a forecast online at www.weather.com. The exact
timing of showers, snow, and sunshine often var-
ies from forecasts, but you can usually expect a
forecasted change sometime within a two-day
margin of error. High-altitude mountain ranges
have their own weather, so be ready for any weather
regardless of the forecast.

❦

Watch cloud formations closely to avoid being
caught at high altitude or on a ridgeline during a
bad storm, especially when lightning is present.

❦

Rain miles away can cause flash floods in canyons,
and you should be especially cautious when hiking in slot canyons.

❦

For more information on weather and on outdoor recreation see *Reading Weather* by Jim Woodmencey (Falcon 1998).

DEALING WITH HEAT

The best way to deal with heat is to drink plenty of water. In a desert or dry, hot climate, wear light-colored clothing and cotton fabrics for hiking during the day. Carry extra water and know where your next water source will be.

❦

Preventing dehydration is safer than treating it. Drink a liter of water or sport drink an hour or two before you reach the trailhead. Then, while hiking drink a mouthful every 20-30 minutes.— Gilbert Preston M.D., *Wilderness First Aid*

❦

On hot days on familiar and good-quality trails, leave in the early morning (or before sunrise) and hike with a headlamp. This early rising practice

allows you to take advantage of the cooler morning.—
George and Rhonda Ostertag, *Hiking New York*

꜀

Always wear a hat, preferably one with a wide brim
all around.

DEALING WITH COLD

The best way to deal with cold is to have the right
clothes, drink lots of liquids, and bring extra fuel
for cooking hot drinks.

꜀

Do not hike too fast; the sweat will make you cold.
Slow down and change wet clothing immediately.

꜀

Travel on snow or ice, even on cloudy days, requires 100 percent UV protection for eyes and a
high level of sunscreen.—Gilbert Preston M.D.,
Wilderness First Aid

꜀

To protect against frostbite, allow enough room in
boots and gloves to avoid blood vessel constric-
tion.—Gilbert Preston M.D., *Wilderness First Aid*

STAYING FOUND

Route-finding, map, compass, and, increasingly, Global Positioning System (GPS) skills are a big part of a safe outdoor adventure. Your primary responsibilities are:
1. Have a map (even if you have GPS, cell phone, etc.).
2. Know how to read the trail and the map with a compass.
3. Know the exact location of your trailhead on the map.

❦

Make sure you start at the right trailhead. If you have the opportunity to check with a ranger in the area before your trip, have him or her mark the correct trailhead on your map.

❦

For safety, always carry a topographic map. The key on the map should tell you the scale. For 7.5-minute quadrangles, the scale is 1:24,000, which means that 1 inch on the map is equivalent to 24,000 inches (2,000 feet) on the ground. Contour intervals give the elevation gain or loss when crossing each line. The most common contour interval is 40 feet, but you may also have maps with

100-, 80-, 50-, or 20-foot intervals. Widely spaced contour lines indicate less elevation change, and closely spaced lines indicate steep terrain. Lines directly on top of each other indicate cliffs.

❧

Do not wait until you are confused to look at your maps. When you start up the trail, begin monitoring your location, so you have a continual fix on your location. Pick out unique landmarks along the way.

❧

To keep from getting lost, orient yourself to natural "handrails"—mountain ridges, valleys, streams, and shorelines—that follow your general line of travel.—Will Harmon, *Hiking Alberta*

❧

Watch for trail markers. Cairns, or "ducks" as they call them in California, are manmade piles of rocks that mark the trail. Blazes are axe marks on trees, often in the form of an upside down exclamation point occurring on opposite faces of a tree trunk. Blazes are not used by management agencies any more, because of damage to the trees.

FINDING YOUR LOCATION
WITH A COMPASS

A compass has an arrow mounted on a baseplate that points to magnetic north. Magnetic north is not real north, but you can adjust for real north by drawing a line extending from and in the direction of the magnetic-north arrow (MN) located on the bottom of your map. Align the compass along this line and turn the map gently until the magnetic arrow lines up with north on the compass.

Use the direction-of-travel arrow on the baseplate or a slotted sighting device to take bearings of two or three landmarks around you. Aim the direction-of-travel arrow at a known landmark, hold the compass steady and level, rotate the dial so that the 0 or magnetic north is lined up exactly with the floating arrow. The corresponding number at the direction-of-travel arrow is the bearing of the landmark. Draw a line on your map on the known landmark in the direction of the bearing (degree).

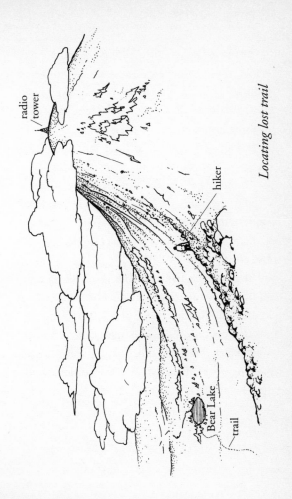

radio
tower

hiker

Bear Lake

trail

Locating lost trail

For example, you are hiking around Mount Defiance and you lose the trail. Fortunately through breaks in the clouds you see Bear Lake and the radio tower on top of the mountain. See "locating lost trail" on the previous page.

Take a bearing for Bear Lake and Mount Defiance and draw lines on the map. See page 49.

If drawn to "known" landmarks at different bearings, the intersection of two lines is your location. For three lines, you are in the triangle, hence the name triangulation. In the example, the two lines cross at a point below the trail on the map, and the trail itself is probably just a short walk uphill. Unfortunately, you do not always have "known" landmarks. If you anticipate hiking off-trail, learn to use GPS and start from a known point. Thick forest and other natural features may interfere with readings, but even an occasional reading is helpful.

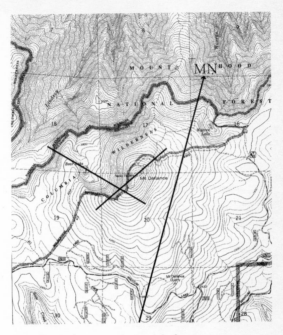

Two lines, drawn on map with degree measurements

USING GPS

A Global Positioning System (GPS) receiver is a navigation device that allows you to locate your position via satellite communication.

⬧

GPS will not help you if you do not know how to read a map.

⬧

GPS is especially useful for expeditions, where your exact location may be a life-or-death matter, and for trail hikes and canoe trips in areas with little elevation change or visible landmarks.

⬧

Learning to use GPS takes practice and, as with many topics, it is a book in itself.

⬧

Take extra batteries for your GPS.

⬧

If you use a Global Positioning System (GPS) receiver to help with backcountry navigation, buy maps preprinted with the metric Universal

Transverse Mercator (UTM) grid, or draw the gridlines yourself before the trip. UTM is much easier to use in the field than latitude and longitude.—Bruce Grubbs, *Hiking Nevada*

IF YOU GET LOST...

If you get lost, do not panic. Sit down and relax for a few minutes while you carefully check your topographic map and take a reading with your compass.

❧

Do not run. If you feel panicked, it will only make you more disoriented and take you farther from the last point of known location.

❧

Confidently plan your next move. It is always smart to retrace your steps until you find familiar ground, even if you think it might lengthen your trip. Many people (even experienced hikers) get temporarily lost in the wilderness but survive by calmly and rationally dealing with the situation.

Should you stay put, or try to walk out? If you can't find your last known location, it's often safest to remain in your current location. There are, however, cases when it is better to try to walk out, such as:

1. Your current location is unsafe.

2. Severe weather is approaching.

3. Nobody knows you are missing, so there is no chance of a search (i.e., you forgot to file your "flight plan").

4. At your location, a rescue signal is unlikely to be seen by rescuers.

5. You do not have enough water or food to survive several days (you can survive without food for a couple of weeks, but you will not make it a week without water).

If you decide to stay put, signal for help. In an open area, build a smoky fire, blow your whistle three times, and yell at the top of your lungs, but do not waste your energy by yelling too much. Spread anything unnaturally colored across the ground or build an SOS to alert air rescue. Do what you can, but keep calm throughout. Most people are rescued within three days.

SHARING

Hikers do not have the trails to themselves. Be the first to yield and give a friendly hello. If you meet a horse party on the trail, move off the trail on the downhill side and quietly let the animals pass. It is too difficult (and sometimes dangerous) for the stock animals to yield. Mountain bikers should yield to hikers, but it is often safer for you to just step off the trail and let a mountain biker pass by.

PACING YOURSELF

Do not exhaust yourself by traveling too far or too fast. Walk as naturally as possible whether going up or downhill. If you get tired, slow down.

⤛

Sing quietly as you walk the trail, especially when hiking alone. If you cannot sing without being out

of breath, then you are overdoing it. Also, be careful not to run off your hiking companions.—
Donna Ikenberry, *Hiking Oregon*

❦

If you have knee problems, consider using lightweight hiking poles.—Donna Ikenberry, *Hiking
Oregon*

❦

Comfortable hiking paces usually vary widely
within larger groups. Rather than limiting the
group to the slowest pace, appoint a rear "caboose"
to sweep the trail and establish checkpoints at
every trail junction so that the group is reformed
often for safety and group control. Each member
of the group should have a map and a clear understanding of the route and destination at the begin-
ning of the day's hike.—Bill Cunningham, *Hiking
California's Desert Parks*

❦

When laboring up a big hill with a big pack, loosen
the chest strap. It allows you to breathe more easily when you need all the breath you can get.

GROUP TRAVEL

Do not hike alone. Every safety and outdoor expert tells you this, but then they take the afternoon to go hiking by themselves. We both hike solo occasionally, but it's clearly safer to travel in groups. If someone is injured, there is someone to go for help. If there are only two people, the victim must be stable to allow the other to go for help; otherwise, he must stay and care for the victim and wait for help. Thus, two people are a little better than one person, so groups of at least three and preferably four people are much safer.

✦

Photocopy maps so each person in the group has one.—Will Harmon, *Wild Country Companion*

GOING SOLO

Definitely leave your itinerary with a friend or relative—where you are going, when you will be back, and how long to wait before going for help.

✦

Do not take chances that you might take with a group.

❦

Bring your survival kit.

❦

Make extra noise in bear country and watch for stalking mountain lions in lion country.

❦

Bring and use your watch. Be realistic about how much time it will take you to get back to where you said you would be at the time you said you would be there.

FORDING RIVERS

Research your hike in advance to make sure it does not involve a ford.

❦

Crossing a river can be safe, but you must know your limits. There are cases where you simply should turn back. Even if only one member of your party (such as a child) might not be able to follow larger, stronger members, you should not try a risky ford.

❦

Be confident. If you are not a strong swimmer, learn to be. Strong swimming skills give you confidence.

❧

Just like getting lost, panic can easily make the situation worse. Another way to build confidence is to practice. Find a small stream and carefully practice crossing it both with a pack and without one.

❧

When you get to a ford, don't automatically cross at the point where the trail comes to the stream. A river can reform each spring during runoff, so a ford that was safe last year might be too deep this year. Study upstream and downstream sections and look for a place where the stream widens and the water is not over waist deep on the shortest member of your party.

❧

Crossing a stream above a logjam can be extremely dangerous. The water flowing beneath the logs may "dive" as it approaches them. The strong current can easily suck the unwary hiker under water beneath the logs from where there may be no escape.—Fred Barstad, *Hiking Oregon's Eagle Cap Wilderness*

CROSSING RIVERS STEP-BY-STEP:

1. Make sure your matches, camera, billfold, clothes, sleeping bag, and any other items you must keep dry are in watertight bags.

2. Have dry clothes ready when you get to the other side to minimize the risk of hypothermia.

3. Do not try a ford with bare feet. Wear hiking boots without socks, sneakers, or tightly strapped sandals.

4. Undo the belt straps on your pack. If you fall in and are washed downstream, a waterlogged pack can anchor you to the bottom. You must be able to easily get out of your pack.

5. Minimize your time in the water, but do not rush; go slowly and deliberately.

6. Take one step at a time. Make sure each foot is securely planted before lifting the other foot. Avoid large slick rocks in favor of gravel beds.

7. Take a 45-degree downstream angle and follow a riffle line if possible.

8. Stay sideways with the current, because turning upstream or downstream increases the force of the current against you. In some cases, two or three people can cross together, locking forearms with the strongest person on the upstream side.

❧

When faced with the choice of crossing on a wet log or fording a stream, wading is the safest choice.—Ron Adkison, *Hiking Grand Canyon National Park*

❧

Carry a stabilizing stick that can also double as a prod for extricating yourself from mud or silt.—Jane and Bert Gildart, *Hiking Shenandoah National Park*

❧

If you have a choice, ford in the early morning when the stream is not as deep. In the mountains, the cool evening temperatures slow snowmelt and reduce the water flow into the rivers. On small streams, a sturdy walking stick used on the up-stream side for balance helps prevent a fall, but in a major river with a fast current, a walking stick offers little help.

❧

If you have to swim, do not panic. Do not try to swim directly across. Instead, pick a long angle and gradually cross to the other side, taking as much as 100 yards or more to get across. If your pack starts to drag you down, get out of it immediately, even if you have to abandon it. If you lose control and are washed downstream, go feet first, so you do not hit your head on rocks or logs.

DEALING WITH DOWNFALL

In burn areas or areas where wet soil and high winds can combine to fell trees, it is impossible for trail crews to clear every downed tree immediately. So, expect to be climbing over a few logs on many trails in the backcountry. In most cases, it is safer to go over logs slowly, without actually stepping on the log. Downfall is often unstable, and putting your weight on it could make it roll or bounce, a sure way to twist an ankle.

❦

If you plan a hike to an area recently burned by forest fires, expect to see many more downed trees.

❦

To save energy when hiking, step over logs rather than stepping up onto a log, then down. Not only will you expend less energy, but in the course of a day, you will take fewer total steps.—Jane and Bert Gildart, *Hiking South Dakota's Black Hills Country*

❦

The only sane way to travel through thick downfall, especially winter lodgepole pine forests, is via state of mind. Peaceful enjoyment of the moment slows you down, keeps the journey safe, and makes it a fun and challenging situation.—Bill Hunger, *Hiking Wyoming*

BLISTERS

The best advice for dealing with blisters is to prevent them. Start with properly fitted boots that are really broken in. Once you know where your rub spots are, place slick tape, either duct or athletic, on high rub areas of your foot. Check for "hot spots" frequently along the trail and apply slick tape or moleskin as needed to reduce rubbing. Be careful with duct tape; some people swear by it, but it can pull off your skin if you are not careful.

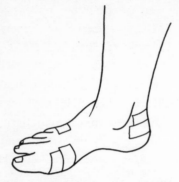

Duct tape on high-rub areas of foot

IF YOU DO GET A BLISTER, **HERE IS WHAT TO DO:**
1. Clean the skin and disinfect with a sterile wipe.
2. After sterilizing scissors, make a small slit.
3. Cover the blister with a gel product like Second Skin (or a Band-Aid will do).
4. Cover the area with moleskin or a moleskin doughnut (opinions differ), and use athletic tape to secure the dressing.

BUGS

The black flies of Maine, the fire ants in Texas, the mosquitoes of Yellowstone, or bugs anywhere can make your trip miserable if you are not prepared—unless you wait until August or September for most of the bugs to die off.

❧

The most common way to deal with biting insects is to spray repellent, usually DEET. Although we know DEET can be harmful, we use it because it is the only thing that really works. Citronella is at best only partially effective. A powerful compromise is to concentrate a DEET application on your clothes, socks, and hat. Avoid direct application to the skin until you just can't take the bugs another minute. Putting DEET on clothing does not work for "fashion" hikers, because DEET eats through plastic and discolors clothing (even more reason not to put it on your skin).

❧

DEET may also help prevent painful but mostly harmless wasp, hornet, yellow jacket, and bee stings. If you are allergic to bee stings, be sure to include an anaphylaxis emergency kit with your personal first-aid kit and consult your doctor before going outdoors.

❧

Bug nets are light, cheap and can be a lifesaver. You can get nets to fit over your hat and face to keep bugs at bay while hiking, and you also can put bug nets over your face while sleeping.

❧

Tuck a bandana into the back brim of a cap to protect the nape of your neck from biting flies and mosquitoes.—Will Harmon, *Hiking Alberta*

❧

Where bugs are abundant, make camp near ridgetops or open slopes where breezes will help hold bugs at bay.—Will Harmon, *Wild Country Companion*

❧

You can also put on your rain gear to prevent bites and stings, but be sure to drink enough liquids to avoid dehydration once you are all bundled up.

TICKS, SNAKES, AND SCORPIONS

Tick season is usually April through June. Unlike other biting insects, ticks do not bite right away; they crawl around and find a nice, warm, hairy spot and dig in. You can prevent bites by wearing long pants and checking your body regularly for ticks, including your head, pubic, and rectal areas.

❦

Tiny deer ticks can cause Lyme Disease. In addition, larger ticks can carry Rocky Mountain Spotted Fever. If you experience flu-like symptoms and/or a spotted or measles-like rash, see a doctor immediately. Both conditions are treatable but fatal if not treated properly.

❦

When hiking in tick-infested areas, it is always a good idea to wear light-colored pants with drawstrings around the ankles, but many of us find shorts to be more comfortable on warm days. If you wear shorts, look at and rub your hands over your bare legs often (every few minutes). You will catch most of the critters this way; they usually land and crawl on your body below the knees.—Fred Barstad, *Hiking Oregon's Eagle Cap Wilderness*

❧

You can duct tape your pants closed around your ankles to prevent tick entry.

❧

Although there are many methods for removing ticks, it is best to use forceps or tweezers, grasp the tick closely around its entire body, and pull straight out, gently and firmly. Afterwards scrub and sterilize the area.

❧

In snake country carry a snakebite kit in your first-aid kit. Neither snakes nor scorpions are aggressive and they only bite or sting in self-defense. When traveling in snake country, do not reach under rocks and crevasses, which are common places for snakes to hide from the hot sun. If you hike or camp in areas known to support poisonous snakes or scorpions, just be cautious and check sleeping bags, boots, and backpacks carefully for uninvited guests.

&

Sleep in a tent with your screen zipped up and you will not wake up with unexpected visitors.

&

Be careful lighting fires. They often drive scorpions from rocks and wood.

&

In areas inhabited by scorpions, always shake out your boots and clothing before putting them on in the morning.—Ron Adkison, *Hiking Wyoming's Wind River Range*

&

If you see a snake or scorpion, stay clear. If you are bitten, stay calm and clean, disinfect the area, and seek medical attention. Many people survive snake and scorpion bites without treatment, but you should consult a physician to increase your survival rate to 100 percent.

WILDLIFE WATCHING

Stay clear of all wild animals. If your viewing an animal changes its natural behavior, you are too close. Disturbing wildlife endangers both wildlife and future wildlife watching. Large hoofed animals can charge when they feel threatened, and this can mean loss of life or limb to you.

❧

Do not feed animals. Feeding by humans can make animals dependent on human food, which lacks the nutrients animals need to build up sufficient fat stores for the winter. Often, this means starvation for fed animals. A fed animal is a dead animal.

❧

Bison look tame, slow, and docile, but the opposite is true in all cases. Always give bison a wide berth.

WATER

Before you leave on a trip, check the distances between water sources. If you have long stretches without access to water, carry extra water.

❧

Because of waterborne microorganisms that can make you sick, even clear mountain water is not safe to drink. Treating water is a necessity.

❦

Filters vary widely in reliability and effectiveness. Buy a model that allows for field cleaning and repair and check consumer reviews.

❦

As an alternative to filters, go with iodine tablets and lemon flavor to cover up the taste. It's much lighter than carrying a filter.

❦

If you have intense diarrhea or vomiting within several weeks of a backpacking trip, see a doctor immediately. Giardiasis and other waterborne illnesses can be life-threatening.

❦

Carry a plastic coffee-filter holder and a few paper coffee filters to screen water before treating it with iodine or a filter. This removes debris before treatment.—Bruce Grubbs, *Hiking Great Basin National Park*

❦

When drawing water from a silty stream, allow water to settle in a collapsible bucket or pan; this will extend the life of your filter.—Ron Adkison, *Hiking California*

❧

In desert canyons, if you expect flooding, treat ample water before flooding. Muddy floodwaters can remain too turbid to use for 8 to 24 hours.—Ron Adkison, *Hiking Grand Canyon National Park*

❧

Since water filters break down, always carry a back-up means of water purification, such as iodine tablets.—Ron Adkison, *Hiking Washington*

TENT SITES

Find a durable surface, at least 100 feet from water and on flat ground. Be wary of bowl-shaped areas and careful of depressions. Do not dig trenches. Instead, pick a spot that will stay dry even under heavy rains.

❧

In bear country, make sure your tent site is at least 100 yards away from your food preparation area and food hanging pole.

❦

When setting up camp under tall trees, look up for "widowmakers," large dead branches and trees that could come crashing down. Widowmakers are especially common in mature ponderosa pine forests.—Bruce Grubbs, *Hiking Oregon's Three Sisters Country*

❦

When backpacking in the desert canyons, always camp above the high water mark, indicated by a line of debris on benches and canyon walls, thus avoiding the potentially fatal results of flash floods.—Ron Adkison, *Hiking California*

❦

DO'S AND DONT'S OF CHOOSING A TENT SITE:
Don't camp on a game or hiking trail.
Don't pitch your tent right next to someone else.
Don't dig trenches or cut branches.
Do put down a ground cloth.
Don't let your ground cloth stretch outside of the fly as it will collect water that will pool up under your tent.

❧

Using a space blanket as a ground cloth can keep your tent warm. On cool nights put the silver reflective side up and set up your tent on it. On warm nights put the red non-reflective side up for a cooler floor.

❧

If you have to set your tent up in the rain, first spread it out, then immediately put your fly over it. Then, push the poles through while keeping the tent under the fly. You can also set up a tarp and then set up the tent under the tarp.

DESIGNATED CAMPSITES

Most national parks and some national forests require backpackers to stay in designated campsites. If so, try to reserve your campsite in advance. This can save you from standing in line at a visitor center once you get there. Before trying to reserve a campsite, however, make sure you have checked the restrictions. Many campsites do not allow campfires, and you won't be able to reserve sites that are closed due to the season and the protection of fragile wildlife resources.

✦

Do not assume that all campsites are easy to find or have a noticeable trailside sign. Vandals knock down and steal signs. Keep the map out. When you get close to the campsite, watch carefully for it, so you do not have to backtrack to find it.

✦

Ask the ranger giving you the permit for specific directions to the campsite, and mark the exact location on your topographic map.

SLEEPING UNDER THE STARS

We have both slept outside of the tent in dry weather but not in areas supporting snakes, scorpions, and bears. You also may weigh the consequences of a wet sleeping bag. If you are sure it is not going to rain, you are not worried about creatures of the night, and you have a warm enough bag, find a soft spot and enjoy a night under the stars.

❧

When you sleep out, use a lightweight bag cover or bivy sac. It will add 10 degrees F of warmth to your sleeping bag and even more if it is breezy.—Bruce Grubbs, *Hiking Nevada*

❧

Just a small draping of mosquito netting that covers the face and is held up by three or four sticks placed upright in the ground around the head can make outside sleeping and star-gazing a summertime possibility.—Bill Hunger, *Hiking Wyoming*

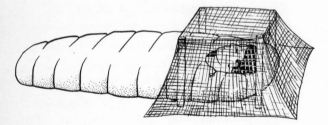

Mosquito net over head for sleeping under the stars

CAMPFIRES

Regulations prohibit campfires in some parts of the backcountry, but if you are in an area where fires are allowed, treat yourself. Besides adding to nightly entertainment, the fire might make your camp safer from bears because you can burn all food scraps and garbage to eliminate food smell.

*

Never plan to use a fire for cooking. If you need warm liquids, use your stove.

*

Avoid building campfires in pristine areas, especially where downed wood is in short supply. Evidence of past campfires invites others to build a fire of their own.—Ron Adkison, *Hiking California*

*

Using an already established fire ring minimizes impact in an area. Moreover, if it is a popular camping spot, leaving that ring clean encourages the next camper to use the same fire ring.—Bill Hunger, *Hiking Wyoming*

❧

Make your own lightweight fire pan by cutting a 2-foot square of flame-retardant canvas from an old discarded wall tent.—Will Harmon, *Hiking Alberta*

❧

For an emergency or wet weather fire starter, carry a single briquette of match-light charcoal wrapped in foil and sealed in a plastic zip-locked bag.—Will Harmon, *Wild Country Companion*

❧

When you cannot find dry wood, look at the base of a spruce.

❧

Building a fire for an emergency is very different than building one on a warm dry night to roast marshmallows. Wet snow can make it hard to find dry wood. You should not break off branches unless it is an emergency. Emergencies take precedence over leave-no-trace concerns.

Almost everyone develops their own way of starting a campfire, but two of the most common methods are the Log Cabin Style and the Teepee Style. Names are intentionally structurally descriptive: you build a log cabin for the first and a teepee for the second, and then you start your fire in the middle. Below are the basics for building an emergency fire and a leave-no-trace fire.

Log Cabin fire

Tepee fire

BUILDING AN EMERGENCY FIRE:

1. Gather all the materials you need to start your fire.

2. Cover your wood with a garbage bag or tarp.

3. Build a small log cabin with 0.25- to 0.5-inch diameter pieces.

4. Take some toilet paper or a paper towel and put it in the middle of the log cabin. Light the paper and feed it with the smallest of dry twigs until it starts to burn the log cabin. If you do not have any small-diameter twigs, use your knife to shave some dry chips. If you are having trouble making the fire go, take a wad of toilet paper and soak it in gas or smear fire paste on it before lighting it in the center of your log cabin.

5. Once the fire is burning, feed it rapidly, especially if it is raining. Once you have the fire burning you can pile logs loosely on top. The smoke will dry them out and then they will burn, and you can repeat the drying and burning process.

6. Be careful to allow space and air in the log cabin. Do not smother it with too much wood at a time, and blow gently to feed the flame.

BUILDING A NO-TRACE FIRE:
1. Gather small-diameter, dead, down wood.
2. With a trowel, dig a 12-inch-diameter pit through organic layers, then set it aside with the top layer intact.
3. Put kindling and paper in the hole and light the fire.
4. Burn only small pieces, less than an inch thick, down to fine white ash.
5. Soak the ashes with water.
6. Replace the soil and make the area look as if no fire occurred.

Before leaving camp the next morning, dig out the fire pit or check the area where you had a fire. Make sure it is cold to the touch and completely out before leaving. Pack out any scorched foil and cans left by other campers.

COOKING

Be careful not to spill on yourself while cooking. If you do, change clothes and hang the clothes with food odor with the food and garbage. Wash your hands thoroughly before retiring to the tent.

❦

Do not cook too much food, so you do not have to deal with leftovers. If you do end up with extra food, carry it out. Don't bury it, throw it in a lake, or leave it. Animals will find and dig up any food or garbage buried in the ground.

❦

If you can have a campfire and decide to cook fish, try cooking them in aluminum-foil envelopes instead of frying them. Then, after removing the cooked fish, quickly and completely burn the fish scraps off the foil. Using foil also means you do not have to wash the pan you used to cook the fish.

❦

Never cook in your tent; you could easily die from carbon monoxide poisoning and, in bear country, you do not want food smell in your tent.

❦

Carry all garbage out.

❦

Prepare for garbage problems before you leave home. Carry in as little garbage as possible by discarding excess packaging while packing. Bring along airtight zip-locked bags to store garbage. Be sure to hang your garbage at night along with your food.

WASHING DISHES

Washing dishes is a sticky problem, but there is one easy solution: if you don't dirty dishes, you don't have to wash them. So, try to minimize food smell by using as few dishes and pans as possible.

❦

Remove food scraps from pans and dishes with paper towels before washing them. Then, when you wash dishes, you have much less food smell.

❦

Burn the dirty towels or store them in zip-locked bags with other garbage.

❦

Put pans and dishes in zip-locked bags before putting them back in your pack.

❦

If you end up with lots of food scraps in the

dishwater, strain out the scraps and store them in zip-locked bags with other garbage.

❦

Do dishes immediately after eating, so a minimum of food smell lingers in the area.

❦

Never wash dishes in a stream or lake and use as little biodegradable soap as possible.

❦

Bring a lightweight screen to filter out food scraps from dishwater, but be sure to store the screen with the food and garbage.

❦

If you have a campfire, pour the dishwater around the edge of the fire. If you don't have a fire or if pouring dishwater on the rocks of the fire is prohibited, take the dishwater at least 100 yards downwind and downhill from camp and pour it on the ground. Do not put dishwater or food scraps in a lake or stream.

❦

Cut a small strip of material from a quick-dry towel. Use it for washing your pot or bowl, then wring it out and use it for drying them.—Donna Ikenberry, *Hiking Colorado's Weminuche Wilderness*

❦

You can skip washing dishes altogether on the last night of your trip. Simply use the paper towels to clean the dirty dishes as much as possible and wash them when you get home. Pack dirty dishes in zip-locked bags before putting them back in your pack.

STORING AND HANGING FOOD

It is best to hang your food. To be as safe as possible, store everything that has any food smell. This includes cooking gear, eating utensils, food bags, garbage, and even clothes with food smells on them. If you take clothes with food smells on them into the tent, you are not separating your sleeping area from food smells.

❦

If the campsite doesn't have a pole or other food storage container, be sure to set one up or at least

locate one before it gets dark. It is not only difficult to store food after dark, but it is easier to miss
a morsel on the ground, and people get hurt while
hanging food in the dark. People often tie a rock
to the string and throw it over the branch, hitting
themselves in the face.

❧

Hang food in airtight, waterproof bags to prevent
food odors from circulating throughout the forest. For double protection, put food and garbage
in zip-locked bags and then seal them tightly in a
larger plastic bag.

❧

The following illustrations depict three popular
methods for hanging food. In any case, try to get
food and garbage at least 10 feet off the ground.

❧

Test the stability of the branch by pulling on both
ends of the strung rope, but do not do this while
standing directly under the branch.

❦

Tie a good knot, wrap the rope around the tree several times, and tie a safety knot. Food coming down during the night can cause animal conflicts and could hurt another party using the same food pole.

❦

Take a special bag for storing food. The bag must be sturdy and waterproof. You can get dry bags at outdoor specialty stores, but you can get by with a trash compactor bag. Regular garbage bags can break and leave your food spread on the ground.

❦

You do not need a heavy climbing rope to store food. Go light instead. Parachute cord will usually suffice unless you plan to hang large quantities of food and gear (which might be the case on a long backpacking excursion or with a large group).

❦

You can buy a small pulley or use a couple of carabiners to make hoisting a heavy load easier.

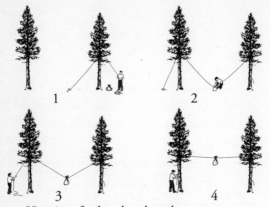

Hanging food and garbage between two trees

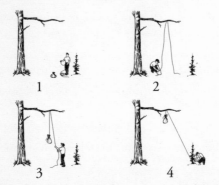

Hanging food and garbage over a tree branch

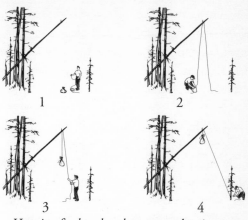

Hanging food and garbage over a leaning tree

The classic method for getting the rope up over a branch or pole is by tying a rock or piece of wood to the end of your rope and tossing it over. Try to use something other than a rock. A rock can easily swing back and hit you in the head. If you carry a carabiner, you can attach the end of your rope to a small stuff sack with a little weight in it. Throw it over and unclip the bag and clip on your food bag.

Use gloves so you don't get rope burns. In addition, of course, do not let the rock or wood come down on your head (it happens!) Also, don't let anybody stand under the bag until you are sure it is securely in place.

※

Once you have untied your food, slowly pull your rope over the branch. Do not jerk it. If the rope is stuck, you may have to leave it behind, unless you can duct tape a knife to a long branch and cut the rope. (You can often score some extra parachute cord left by others with this retrieval method.)

※

Smaller rodents and flying squirrels can also be a problem. Many heavily used areas have food storage areas; take advantage of these if required and if they appear to work. If the managing agency has provided a food storage device, use it instead of hanging food.

※

In desert areas or places where large mammals are not present, rodents and small mammals are the biggest threat to your food supply. To keep them out of your food, hang your food at least 4 feet off the ground with 20- to 30-pound test monofilament fishing line. Rodents can easily climb nylon cord to reach your food, but not slippery fishing line.—Ron Adkison, *Hiking California*

THE WILDERNESS RESTROOM

Many an uncomfortable conversation in the backcountry surrounds the basic function of going to the bathroom. There is no bathroom at most backcountry sites, but in heavy-use areas, use existing facilities. When you do not have a toilet, urinate at lease 200 feet from water.

❧

Constipation is common on backcountry trips. Prepare meals with high-fiber lentils, beans, and dried fruit to maintain normal bowel functioning.—Gilbert Preston M.D., *Wilderness First Aid*

❧

For alpine ascents or heavily used areas, consider a "poop tube," (a 4-inch diameter piece of PVC pipe

AS FAR AS GETTING RID OF SOLID HUMAN WASTE, HERE ARE THE BASICS:

1. Find a secluded spot at least 200 feet from water.
2. Dig a hole at least 6 inches deep.
3. Drop your drawers.
4. Squat down, using an arm for support or a log if you picked a good spot.
5. Relax, do your business.
6. Fill the hole with the dirt and sod; try to make it look like there was never a hole.

capped at one end and threaded for a screw-on lid on the other end) and pack out all solid waste.

❦

Be sure to check local regulations for restrictions on the disposal of human waste. And, to avoid more restrictive regulations, be extra careful with waste.

FOR WOMEN

It is generally accepted that if buried, the secretions of menstruation in tampons or pads will attract—and be dug up by—wild animals. In some cases, there might be pit toilets in the backcountry, where disposal is allowed, but in most cases, plan on packing them out with the rest of your garbage.

❦

Store used feminine hygiene products in double-bagged, zip-locked bag. This will probably be the first thing you want to dispose of in a designated receptacle when you reach the trailhead. Use sanitary wipes for cleaning hands. Pack these out with used tampons and pads.

MEDICAL EMERGENCIES

Wilderness first aid is a book in itself. In most cases, you cannot just call 911 until you get back to the trailhead or a local town. Then, an ambulance cannot always drive right to you, and often, rural wilderness areas have limited medical facilities. A sensible minimum precaution is to take a course on first aid and CPR. Neither this book nor any other book can teach you how to react to all emergencies, but a few guidelines are offered on the next page:

HANDLING EMERGENCIES STEP-BY-STEP:
1. Make sure the scene is safe before approaching an injured person.
2. Do not move the victim; stabilize the head and neck.
3. If the victim is conscious, ask about his or her condition.
4. If the victim is unconscious, check ABCs (airway, breathing, circulation or pulse), and any external injuries. Administer CPR if needed.
5. Apply pressure to stop any external bleeding.
6. Check the head and neck for injuries.
7. Monitor for shock.
8. Get help for any serious injuries where self-evacuation could cause more damage.

❦

If you encounter an accident victim on the trail, first calm down, then evaluate the scene and check ABCs: airway, breathing, and circulation.—Gilbert Preston M.D., *Wilderness First Aid*

❦

A conscious victim must grant permission before you can administer first aid.

＊

To be really well prepared for backcountry accidents, take a Wilderness First Responder Course.—Gilbert Preston M.D., *Wilderness First Aid*

＊

Diabetics should carry all needed sugar and insulin supplies, and be sure other members of their party know where the supplies are and what signs to look for when they are needed.

＊

To treat insulin shock, the diabetic, and all members of his or her group should carry an instant form of glucose, such as packets of sugar, or a package of cake frosting.—Gilbert Preston, M.D., *Wilderness First Aid*

＊

For more information on handling wilderness medical emergencies consult the book *Wilderness First Aid* by Gilbert Preston, M.D. (Falcon 1997).

ALTITUDE

Above 8,000 feet, altitude can cause problems for any outdoor adventure. Altitude illness can be life-threatening, but it has a simple cure—get to a lower altitude. If you or a companion experience headaches, loss of appetite, loss of energy, nausea, difficulty sleeping, and/or low urine output, descend 2,000 to 4,000 feet as soon as possible. If someone cannot get to a lower altitude alone, help them. Never leave someone who has symptoms of altitude illness.

❦

Be advised that above 10,000 feet elevation the oxygen amount in the air diminishes, and one's pace must often be slowed to accommodate that fact.—Bill Hunger, *Hiking Wyoming*

❦

Drink lots of water. $C^2 P^2$ = Clean and Copious Pee Pee

❦

Carry throat lozenges on high-altitude trips for sore raspy throat caused by dry air and increased rate of breathing.—Gilbert Preston M.D., *Wilderness First Aid*

HYPOTHERMIA

Be aware of the danger of hypothermia, a condition in which the internal temperature of the body drops below normal. It can lead to mental and physical collapse and death. With full-blown hypothermia, as energy reserves are exhausted, cold reaches the brain, depriving you of good judgment and reasoning power. You won't be aware that this is happening. You lose control of your hands. Your internal temperature slides downward. Without treatment, this slide leads to stupor, collapse, and death.

If your party is exposed to wind, cold, and wet, think hypothermia. Watch yourself and others for these symptoms: uncontrollable fits of shivering; vague, slow, slurred speech; memory lapses; incoherence; immobile, fumbling hands; frequent stumbling or a lurching gait; drowsiness (to sleep is to die); apparent exhaustion; and inability to get up after a rest. When a member of your party has hypothermia, he or she may deny any problem. Believe the symptoms, not the victim.

❦

To defend yourself against hypothermia, stay dry. When clothes get wet, they lose about 90 percent of their insulating value. Wool loses relatively less heat. Cotton, down, and some synthetics lose more. Choose rain clothes that cover the head, neck, body, and legs and provide good protection against wind-driven rain. Most hypothermia cases develop in air temperatures between 30 and 50 degrees F, but hypothermia can develop in warmer temperatures. Also, dress in layers, drink lots of water, and eat foods high in carbohydrates and fats while engaged in strenuous outdoor exercise.

❦

For mild, but possible wet weather camping, fleece sleeping bag liners greatly increase the temperature range of a synthetic sleeping bag.—Fred Barstad, *Hiking Oregon's Mount Hood and Badger Creek Wilderness*

✍

If you get cold, warm up before you get colder. Remove wet clothing, keep moving, eat something, move your arms in circles to get blood to your fingertips, and if you have to, set up your tent and get in your sleeping bag.—Donna Ikenberry, *Hiking Oregon*

✍

Set up camp early to avoid exposure to nighttime temperatures.

✍

Exposure to cold, moisture, wind, dehydration, and exhaustion all cause hypothermia. The moment you begin to lose heat faster than your body produces it, you're suffering from exposure. Your body starts involuntary exercise, such as shivering, to stay warm and makes involuntary adjustments to preserve normal temperature in vital organs, restricting blood flow in the extremities. Both responses drain your energy reserves. The only way to stop the drain is to reduce the degree of exposure.

TREAT HYPOTHERMIA AS FOLLOWS:
Get the victim out of the wind and rain.
Strip off wet clothes.
If the victim is only mildly impaired, give him or her warm drinks. Then get the victim in warm clothes and a warm sleeping bag. Place well-wrapped water bottles filled with heated water close to the victim.
If the victim is badly impaired, attempt to keep him or her awake. Put the victim in a sleeping bag with another person. If you have a double bag, put two warm people in with the victim.

❧

LIGHTNING

The high altitude topography of the backcountry is prone to sudden thunderstorms, especially in July and August. If a lightning storm catches you, take special precautions.

❧

Lightning can travel far ahead of the storm, so be sure to take cover before the storm hits.

❧

Don't try to make it back to your vehicle or to your chosen campsite. It is not worth the risk. Instead, seek shelter even if it is only a short way back to the trailhead. Lightning storms usually don't last long, and from a safe vantage point, you might enjoy the sights and sounds.

❧

Be especially careful not to be caught on a mountaintop or exposed ridge, under large, solitary trees, in the open, or near standing water.

❧

Seek shelter in a low-lying area, ideally in a dense stand of small, uniformly sized trees.

❧

Stay away from anything that might attract lightning, such as metal tent poles, graphite fishing rods, or pack frames.

❧

Get in a crouched position and place both feet firmly on the ground.

❦

If you have a pack (without a metal frame) or a sleeping pad with you, put your feet on it for extra insulation against shock.

❦

Do not walk or huddle together. Instead, stay 100 feet apart, so if lightning strikes somebody in your group, others in your party can give first aid.

❦

If you are in a tent, stay there, in your sleeping bag with your feet on your sleeping pad.

❦

Despite the common myth, a person struck by lightning cannot electrocute you.—Gilbert Preston, M.D., *Wilderness First Aid*

BE MOUNTAIN LION ALERT

Mountain lions are rarely seen, but when they are, it is often a dangerous situation. The best advice is to avoid hiking, running, or biking alone in lion country. For more information read *Mountain Lion Alert* by Steven Torres (Falcon 1997).

❦

IF YOU SEE A MOUNTAIN LION:
Remain calm.
Look big, raise your arms, puff your chest, and look as intimidating as possible. Do not hunch over or crouch, which makes you appear to be a smaller target. Keep your pack on.
If the lion attacks, fight with everything you have. Many attacks have been successfully warded off by aggressive response. Use a pocketknife, stick, fishing rod case, rock, and anything else to fight back.
Report all mountain lion sightings to a ranger.

❦

BE BEAR AWARE

The first step of any hike in bear country is an attitude adjustment. Nothing guarantees total safety. Hiking in bear country adds a small additional risk to your trip. However, that risk can be greatly minimized by adhering to this age-old piece of advice—be prepared. Moreover, being prepared does not only mean having the right equipment.

THE BEAR ESSENTIALS OF
HIKING AND CAMPING:

Knowledge is the best defense.

There is no substitute for being alert.

Hike with a large group and stay together.

Do not hike alone in bear country.

Stay on the trail.

Hike in the middle of the day.

Make lots of noise while hiking.

Never approach a bear.

Females with cubs are very dangerous.

Stay away from carcasses.

Keep separate sleeping and cooking areas.

Sleep in a tent.

Cook just the right amount of food and eat it all.

Store food and garbage out of reach of bears.

Never feed bears.

Keep food odors out of the tent.

Leave the campsite cleaner than you found it.

Leave no food rewards for bears.

Report all bear sightings to a ranger.

It also means having the right information. Knowledge is your best defense. For more information on bear safety, read *Bear Aware* by Bill Schneider (Falcon 1996).

⤛

Use your knowledge of bear habitat and habits: be especially alert in areas most likely to be frequented by bears. This includes areas such as avalanche chutes, berry patches, streams, stands of whitebark pine, and high wind or high noise areas.

⤛

There is safety in numbers: there have been very few instances where a large group has had an encounter with a bear.

Leave No Trace

Going into the wilderness is like visiting a famous museum. You do not want to leave your mark on an art treasure in a museum. If everybody going through a museum left one little mark, the contents of the museum would quickly be destroyed, and of what value is a big building full of trashed art? The same goes for a pristine wilderness such as the backcountry, which is as magnificent as any masterpiece by any artist. If we all left just one little mark on the landscape, the wilderness would soon be despoiled.

A wilderness can accommodate human use as long as everybody behaves. However, a few thoughtless or uninformed visitors can ruin it for everybody who follows. All wilderness users have a responsibility to know and follow the rules of no-trace camping. Canoeists can look behind the canoe and see no trace of their passing. Hikers, mountain bikers, horse packers, and four-wheelers should have the same goal. Enjoy the wilderness, but leave no trace of your visit. An important source of these guidelines is in the book *Leave No Trace* by Will Harmon (Falcon 1997).

THREE FALCON PRINCIPLES OF LEAVE NO TRACE
- *Leave with everything you brought in.*
- *Leave no sign of your visit.*
- *Leave the landscape as you found it.*

Most of us know better than to litter in or out of the wilderness. Be sure you leave nothing, regardless of how small it is, along the trail or at the campsite. This means you should pack out everything, including orange peels, flip tops, cigarette butts, and gum wrappers. Also, pick up any trash that others leave.

After practicing the principles of Leave No Trace, put your ear to the ground in the wilderness, and listen carefully. Thousands of people coming behind you are thanking you for your courtesy and good sense.

LEAVE NO TRACE STEP-BY-STEP:
Follow the main trail.
Avoid cutting switchbacks and walking on vegetation beside the trail.
Don't pick up souvenirs, such as rocks, antlers, or wildflowers. The next person wants to see them, too, and collecting such souvenirs is often illegal.
Remember, sound travels easily to the other side of a lake. Be courteous.
Carry a lightweight trowel to bury human waste and pack out used toilet paper.
Keep human waste at least 200 feet from any water source.
Strictly follow the pack-in/pack-out rule. If you carry something into the backcountry, consume it or carry it out.

Carry a readily available plastic bag for trash you encounter on the trail.—Polly Burke, *Wild Utah*

Helping Management Agencies

For your safety and the safety of other wilderness travelers, you should report all trail dangers to the local ranger district. This includes any wild animal confrontations, bears eating garbage, habituated deer, dangerous fords, washed out trails, and illegal human activity. It is up to us to make managing public lands easy for agencies, by obeying local regulations, picking up garbage along the trail, and practicing leave-no-trace ethics. Doing these things will ensure that our children get to see the same wild lands we did, untrammeled and pristine.

Send in Your Tips

The authors who submitted tips for this book have thousands of miles of trail experience, but every person who hikes knows there are many ways to do something right. Your way, as long as it is safe and low impact, is the way for you. We invite you to experiment, find ways to reduce weight, eat better, and travel safer. Then, share them with us and we will share them with everybody.

Falcon continually updates all FalconGuides. We invite you to contribute to the next edition of Backpacking Tips. If your tips make the next edition, you will receive a free FalconGuide, courtesy of Falcon. If you wish to send in tips for the next edition of Backpacking Tips, please write or e-mail:

Backpacking Tips
c/o Falcon Publishing
P.O. Box 1718
Helena, MT 59624
Falconbk@ixnet.com

Appendix A

FALCONGUIDES BY THE CONTRIBUTORS

Ron Adkison *Hiking California, Hiking Washington, Hiking Wyoming's Wind River Range, Hiking Grand Canyon National Park, Best Easy Dayhikes Glen Canyon, Best Easy Dayhikes Grand Canyon*

Fred Barstad *Hiking Oregon's Mount Hood and Badger Creek, Hiking Oregon's Eagle Cap Wilderness*

Polly Burke *Wild Utah, Hiking California's Desert Parks*

Bill Cunningham *Wild Montana, Wild Utah, Hiking California's Desert Parks*

Bert and Jane Gildart *Hiking South Dakota's Black Hills Country, Best Easy Dayhike Shenandoah, Hiking Shenandoah*

Bruce Grubbs *Hiking Great Basin National Park, Hiking Nevada, Hiking Oregon's Three Sisters Country, Hiking Northern Arizona*

Will Harmon *Leave No Trace, Hiking Alberta, Wild Country Companion, Mountain Biking Helena, Fat/Trax Bozeman*

Bill Hunger *Hiking Wyoming, Best Hikes along the Continental Divide*

George and Rhonda Ostertag *Hiking Pennsylvania, Hiking New York, Hiking Southern New England*

Gilbert Preston, M.D. *Wilderness First Aid*

Bill Schneider *Hiking Montana, Bear Aware, Hiking the Beartooth, Hiking Yellowstone National Park, Hiking Guadelupe and Carlsbad Caverns National Parks, Exploring Canyonlands, Best Easy Dayhikes Beartooths, Best Easy Dayhikes Canyonlands, Best Easy Dayhikes Yellowstone, Best Hikes along the Continental Divide*

Russ Schneider *Hiking the Columbia River Gorge, Fishing Glacier National Park, Best Hikes along the Continental Divide, The Wilderness Directory*

Appendix B

Probably the best way to make sure you have everything you need before a trip is to have a checklist.

❧

The best place to store your checklist is in the top pocket of your pack, so you can take notes for the next time.—Bill Hunger, *Hiking Wyoming*

❧

Although standardized checklists are helpful, each person should develop his or her own personalized checklist derived from experience hiking in different seasons and trip duration. Keep good notes during each trip of what works and what doesn't work for you, in order to refine your personal pretrip checklist.—Bill Cunningham, *Wild Utah*

❧

The following pages are lists of essential gear for both day hiking and backpacking, and a list of recommended gear for comfort and pleasure. Keep weight in mind during all of your trip planning. Consider these checklists a guide only; you should carefully consider each item you take. All of these checklists are designed for groups of three people, as hiking solo is not recommended. Rememeber to keep extra food, water, and clothing in the car.

TABLE 1: DAY-HIKING CHECKLIST

For day hiking wear baggy shorts, trail-running shoes or boots, synthetic socks, T-shirt, and your favorite hiking hat. You can go as light as just an extra shell, water, snacks, and survival kit, but it helps to carry other comfort and and safety items. Bill also carries binoculars, a camera, film, and fishing gear. Russ often adds fishing gear and field guides.

Individual Items	Weight (oz.)
One-liter water bottle (full of water)	36
Day pack	48
Extra clothing: rain pants, rain jacket, wool gloves, stocking cap, wool or synthetic sweater (may vary with climate)	86
Survival kit (from "The Backpacking Essentials" list)	20.5

Map (a copy for each person)	3.5
Money, credit card, driver's license	2
Sunglasses (in breakproof case)	3
Weight of individual items	**199 oz.**

Group Items (for three hikers)	Weight (oz.)
Water filter (carry backup iodine, too)	19
Plastic trowel, toilet paper	10
Bug repellent in sealed plastic bag	2
Keys (attached to inside of pack)	3
Snacks	20
Sunscreen	2
Headlamp (with fresh batteries)	8.5
First-aid kit (from "The Backpacking Essentials")	27.3

Weight of group items   91.8 oz.   (30.6 oz./person)
Weight of day hiking items (per hiker)   229.6 oz.
   (14.3 lbs.)

TABLE 2: THE BACKPACKING ESSENTIALS

The list below represents a basic checklist for a three-day, two-night backpack for three people. If you go by yourself, you will need to shave off a few pounds, most likely with a lighter tent and less cookware.

The checklist starts with items that all parties should carry, then adds in their percentage of the group's weight if the group items are divided equally. Food is not listed as a group item, because each person would carry the same amount of food with or without a group. The list includes articles of clothing you wear on the first day, and hence have to carry the rest of the trip.

Individual Items	Weight (oz.)
One-liter water bottle (full of water)	36
Lighweight Backpack (internal frame, doubles as partial emergency sleeping shell)	72
Synthetic sleeping bag (20 degree F rating, in a garbage bag and stuffed into a stuff sack)	61
Pack fly or poncho (to cover pack while hiking and while breaking camp; can also be used as a ground cloth)	12
Foam sleeping pad	9
Heavy-duty garbage bags or trash compactor bags	6
Clothing	
Baggy hiking shorts	6
Hiking hat (with brim)	3

Knit hat (wool or synthetic)	4
Trail hiking shoes	48
Polypropylene long underwear (tops and bottoms)	12
Underwear (at least two sets)	12
Rain pants	22
Waterproof or rubberized rain jacket	36
Wool or synthetic gloves	2
Wool or synthetic socks (1 pair)	8
Wool sweater (or synthetic insulated jacket)	22
Cotton socks (2 pair)	12

Survival Kit

Candle	1
Cigarette lighters (2, in waterproof wrapper)	2
Compass with signal mirror	2
Emergency fire starter in film case	1.5
Emergency food bars (2)	5
Iodine tablets (backup)	1.5
Matches (with strike strip in waterproof container)	1.2
Plastic whistle	0.8
Space blanket	2
Pocket knife	3.5

Top of Pack (survival/safety items continued)

Bug repellent in sealed bag	2
Duct tape (partial roll on pencil)	1
Extra batteries (4 AA)	4

Extra bulbs in film case	2
Headlamp (with fresh batteries)	8.5
Keys (attached to inside of pack)	3
Map (each member of group should have a copy)	3.5
Money, credit card, driver's license	2
Sunglasses (in breakproof case)	3
Sunscreen	2
Plastic trowel and toilet paper and any needed feminine hygiene products	10
Waterproof journal and pencil	4
Toothbrush and toothpaste	4

Food (per person—85 oz. total)

Drink Bag: 6 tea bags, 3 apple cider packets, 6 soup packets, 5 lemon-flavor packets	10
Snacks/Breakfast: 6 breakfast bars, 2 cups trail mix, bag of almonds, 3 boxes raisins	37
Meal Bag 1: baguette and 12 oz. sharp cheddar cheese	23
Meal Bag 2: Noodles and sauce or rice and sauce dinners	12
Insulated plastic cup with lid	3
Plastic spoon and fork	1.5

Weight of individual items	**539 oz. (33.7 lbs.)**

Group Items	**Weight (oz.)**
Camp stove (with cigarette lighter)	24
Fuel bottle (full of gas, 32 oz., may vary with fuel efficiency of stove)	29
Pans (2 pans, lids, handles)	21
Pepper spray (in bear country)	16
50 feet of cord	4
Tent (three person)	91
Water filter (carry backup iodine in personal survival kit)	19
Permit (if required)	0.1
First-aid Kit	
Ace bandage	2.5
Adhesive bandages (Band-Aids®)	1.5
Adhesive tape (1 roll)	3
Antibiotic ointment packets (or small tube of Neosporin)	0.5
Cravat (triangular bandage)	1.8
Gauze pads (four, 4" x 4")	1.6
Gauze rollers	2
Medications (laxative, anti-diarrhea, allergy, aspirin, ibuprofen)	2
Nonadhesive bandage (for burns)	0.5
Nylon bag	4

Rubber/vinyl gloves (2 pair)	1.4
Safety pins	0.5
Scissors	3
Tweezers (forceps)	0.5
Wound closure strips	0.5
Moleskin or Molefoam pieces	2

Weight of group items	231.4 (77.1 oz. per person)
Weight per person	616.1 oz.
	(38.5 lbs.)

Note: If you have any special conditions or allergies (such as bee stings), you should consult with your physician before taking a backpacking trip. If you are allergic to bee stings, carry an anaphylaxis emergency kit. If you are diabetic, be sure to include necessary insulin and glucose paste for emergencies. If you are traveling in snake country, be sure to carry a snakebite kit. For more information on wilderness first-aid kits see *Wilderness First Aid* by Gilbert Preston, M.D. (Falcon 1997).

TABLE 3: BACKPACKING EXTRAS

If you fish, like to eat well in the woods, appreciate a tarp in the rain, like an inflated mattress, fancy utility tools, and the like, then you may need more than the "Backpacking Essentials." In a sense, backpacking is about pleasure, and different people choose different luxuries in the backcountry. You may want a bottle of wine or a float tube for fishing or fresh veggies and eggs. You can have these, but they come with a price, a price in weight.

These are items you might add or replace with lighter items for guiding, teaching seminars, photographing remote areas, or going on backcountry fishing trips. You don't need to carry every one of the items listed, but we have included most of these items in our packs on more than one occasion, and it is conceivable that you could take them all.

Fancy Food	**Weight (oz.)**
Plastic spoon, fork, and knife	3
Plastic bowl	2

Fancy Food (continued)	**Weight (oz.)**

Drinks: 6 tea bags, 3 apple cider packets,
  2 hot-chocolate packets, 4 soup packets, 5 lemon-flavor
  packets, fresh-ground coffee, powdered milk, sugar
  packets   16

Breakfasts: Whole wheat pancake mix, butter,
  and syrup in sealed containers; dried hash browns
  (mixed with onions and dried veggies, dehydrated
  salsa, and cheese.)   24

Snacks: 6 breakfast bars, 2 cups trail mix,
  1 cup almonds   17

Lunches: Sausage, cheese, crackers (first day
  deli lunch at car and deli lunch in cooler
  at pickup point or left with lots of ice in car)   27

Dinners: 1: Home-mixed dried chili (dried corn,
  pre-cooked and dried beans, onion, pepper, chili
  powder, and dehydrated salsa); 2: Spaghetti—
  noodles and powdered spaghetti sauce (basil,
  oregano, garlic, pepper, dried onion, dried
  mushrooms, dried zucchini, chili powder,
  bulk dried tomato powder), fresh parmesan.
  Extra: pre-folded aluminum pocket for cooking
  fish and onion, and mushroom cup-of-soup   26

Tortillas and garlic bread   32

Spice kit: Dehydrated salsa, pepper, and garlic   4

Fishing stuff	**Weight (oz.)**
Fanny pack, flies, reel, extra spool with wet line, bug dope, hemostats, bug net, extra leader and tippet material, dry-fly floatant	38
Flyrod in aluminum rod case (doubles as walking/ wading stick)	22

Cook Kit	**Weight (oz.)**
Biodegradable soap	2
Hot pads	2
Pans (3, lids, dipping cup, nylon bag)	56
Paper towels	8
Coffee cone/filters	3
Plastic spoon, fork, knife	3
Screen (for filtering dishwater)	1
Scrubby (rough plastic dish sponge)	1

First-aid Kit	**Weight (oz.)**
Cortisone anti-itch cream	2
Cotton balls	0.6
CPR face shield	1
First-aid book	2
Inhaler	3.2
Plastic airway device	0.6
Splinting material	3

First-aid Kit (continued)	Weight (oz.)
Sterile wipes	1.5
Wash buckets (2)	16
Fuel bottle (full of gas, 32 oz.; may vary with fuel efficiency of stove)	28
Carabiner (for hanging extra heavy pack or attaching stuff)	3
Lightweight nylon tarp (with parachute cord attached)	18
Nylon rope (50 feet or more)	14
Camera and extra film	10
Chest harness for camera	5
Binoculars	14
Backup water filter	19
Guidebook in plastic bag	12

Blister Kit	Weight (oz.)
Bottle of New Skin ™	3
Second Skin pieces	1
Moleskin or Molefoam ™ pieces	2
Sterile wipes	1
Micra ™ utility tool with scissors and tweezers	3

Appendix C

Once you get to the trailhead and change clothes, stop at a pizza place, and grab a cold beverage, don't forget your post-trip duties. It is in your best interest to do a little post-trip maintenance, especially if your trip has been a dirty one. Probably the most important thing you can do to preserve your gear is to make sure it is clean and dry before storing it.

❑ Call or notify those you left word with of your itinerary. This way they know you got back safely and won't call for a massive search. An unwanted search for someone who it not lost is costly and embarrassing.

❑ For your safety and the safety of other wilderness travelers, you should report all trail dangers to the local ranger district.

❏ Clean all gear and repair any items damaged during the trip, so you're ready for the next trip.

❏ Take your sleeping bag out of the stuff-sack and put it loosely in a storage bag.

❏ Dry out your tent, fly and rain gear before storing.

❏ Dump your garbage, but don't fill trailhead garbage cans. Drive it in. Drive it out

Replenish survival and first-aid items used unexpectedly, so you don't forget them on the next trip.

About the Editors

Bill Schneider

Bill Schneider has spent more than thirty years hiking trails all across America. During college in the mid-1960s, he worked on a trail crew in Glacier National Park. He spent the 1970s publishing the Montana Outdoors magazine for the Montana Department of Fish, Wildlife & Parks and covering as many miles of trails as possible on weekends and holidays. In 1979, Bill and his partner, Mike Sample, created Falcon Publishing, and released two guidebooks their first year. Bill wrote one of them, *Hiking Montana*. Since then he has written many other books and articles on wildlife, outdoor recreation, and environmental issues. Bill has also taught classes on bicycling, backpacking, no-trace camping, and hiking in bear country for the Yellowstone Institute, a nonprofit educational organization in Yellowstone National Park. Today Bill is president of Falcon Publishing, which is the premier publisher of outdoor recreation guidebooks with more than 400 titles in print.

Russ Schneider
Since 1993, Russ has been a backpacking, rafting, and fishing guide with Glacier Wilderness Guide in West Glacier, Montana. He also serves as editor for Falcon's how-to books. He is currently continuing to guide and compiling the *Wilderness Directory* for Falcon. As Bill's son he has benefitted from many hiking trips over the years and now carries most of the weight when they backpack together. He was seven years old in the original cover photo of *Hiking Montana*. They are currently working on the twentieth anniversary edition of *Hiking Montana*.

Hiking